sniff shout

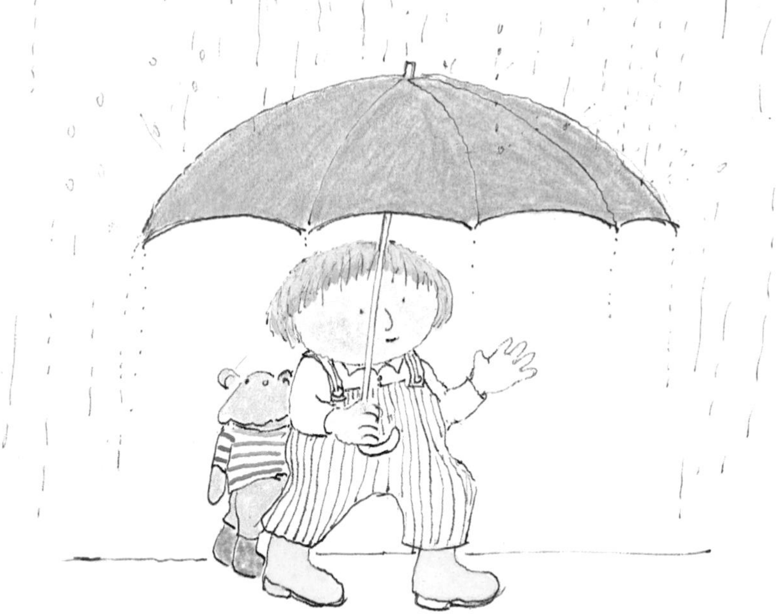

John Burningham

WALKER BOOKS
LONDON

suck

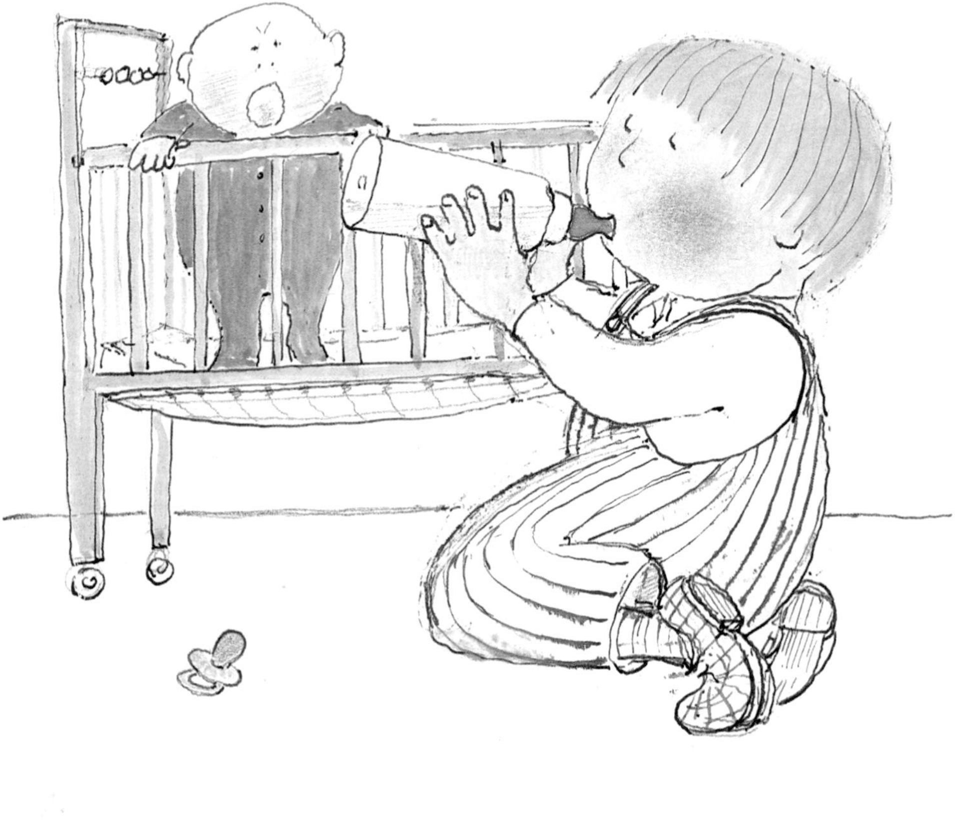

slurp

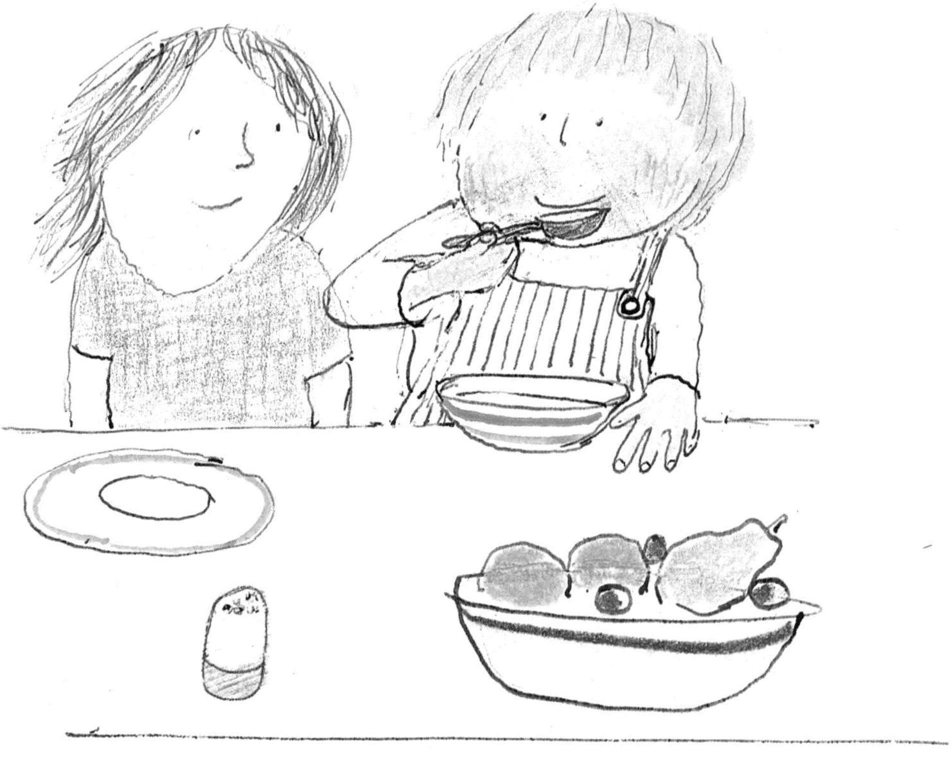

shout

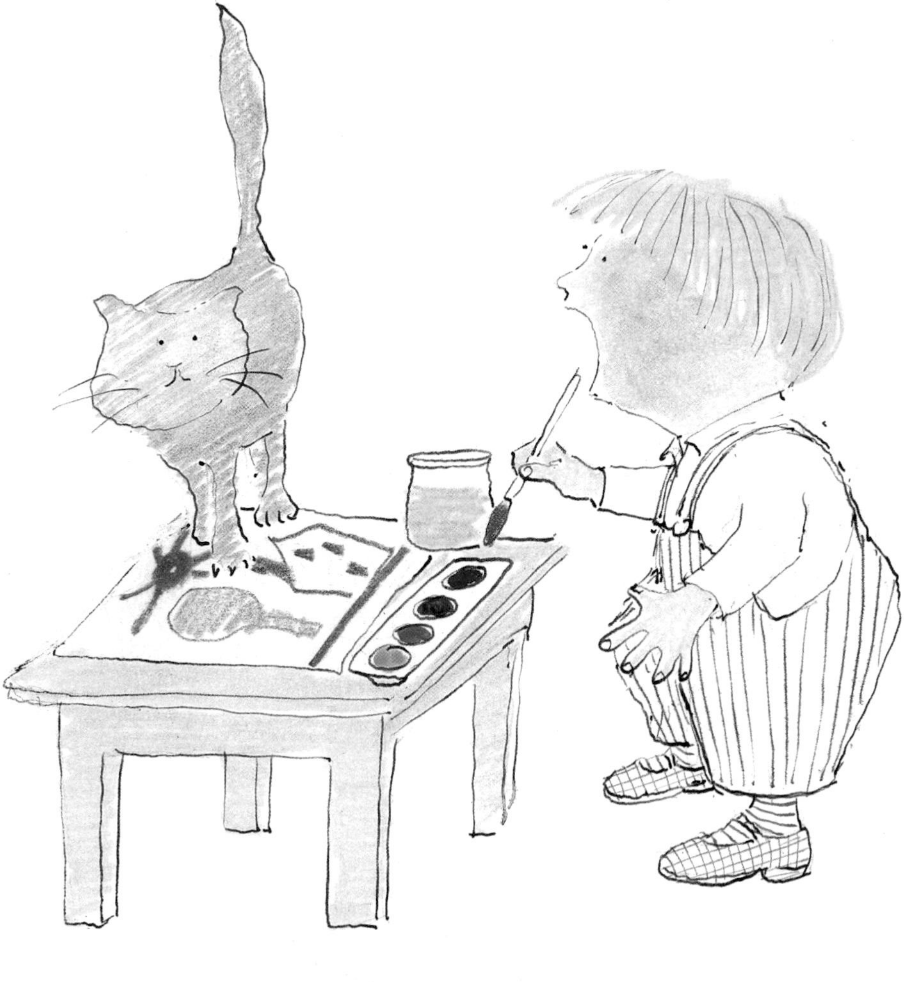

sob

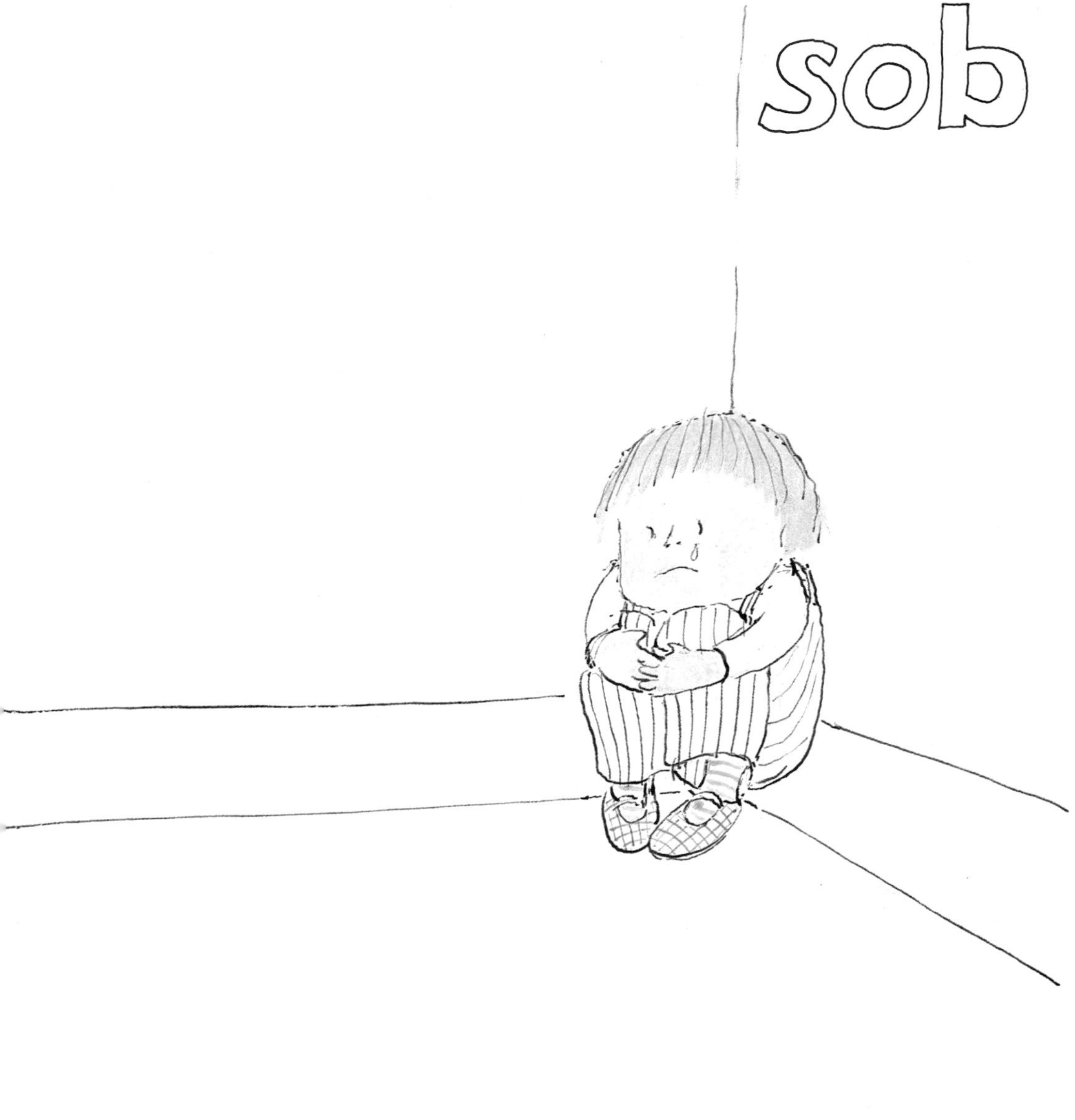

cough

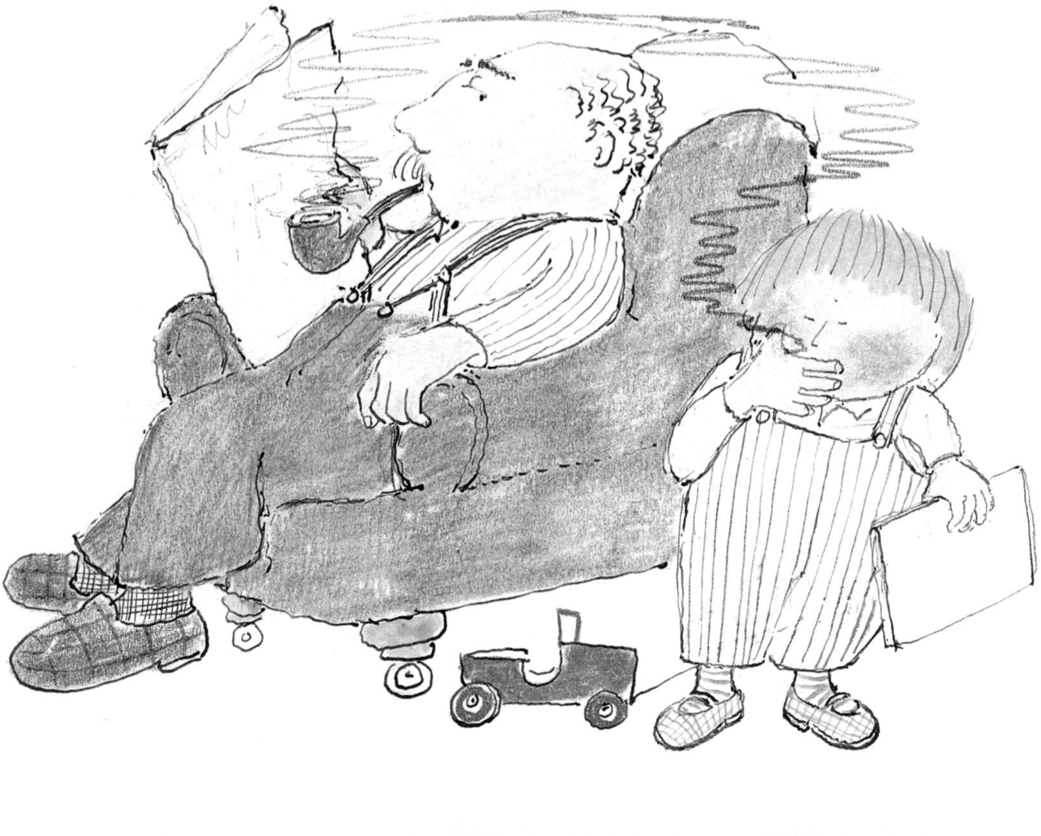

Snore

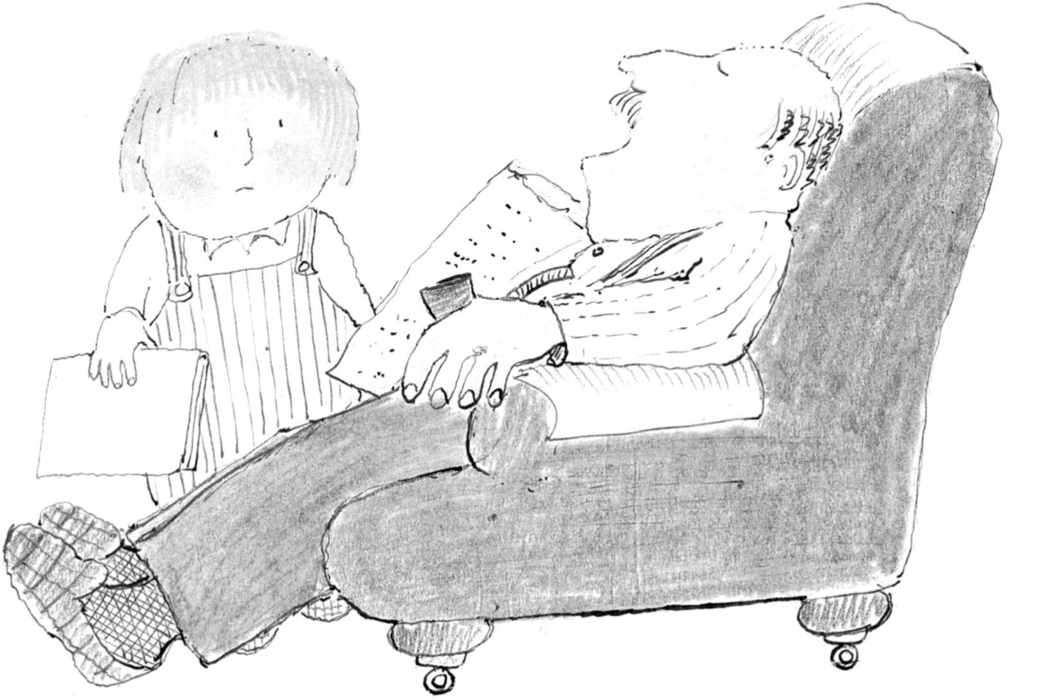

sniff

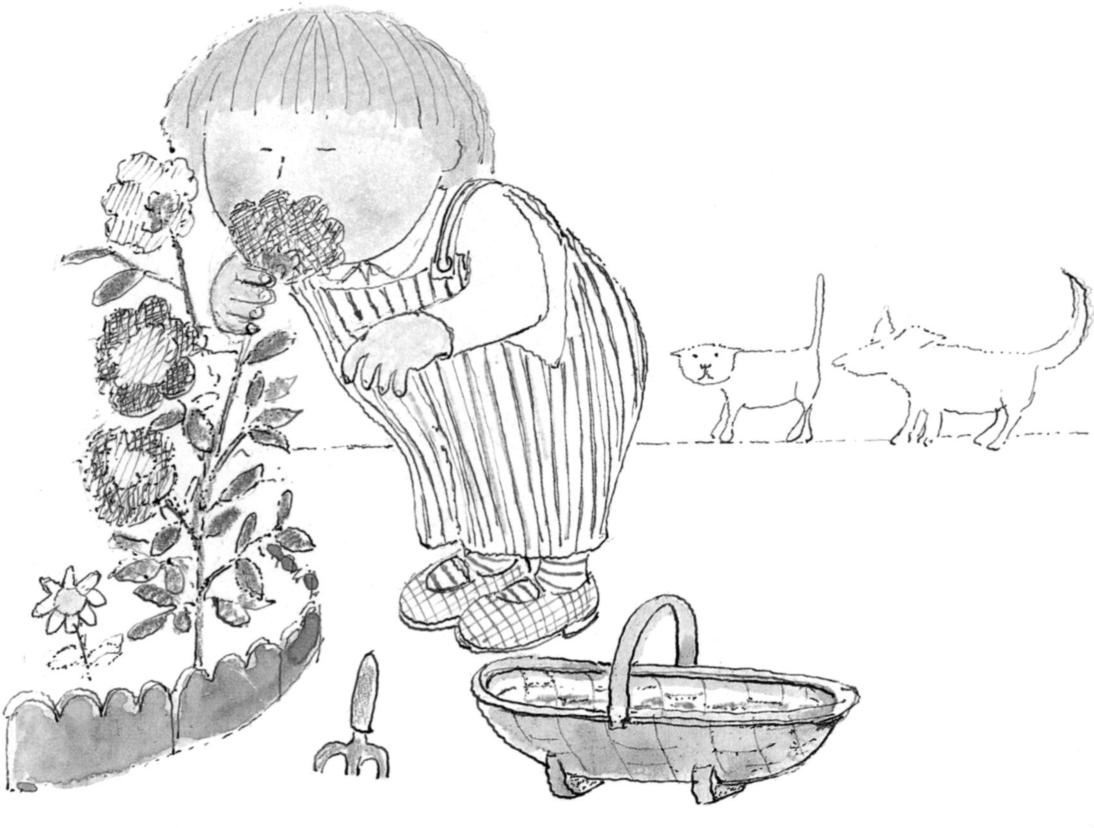

Sneeze

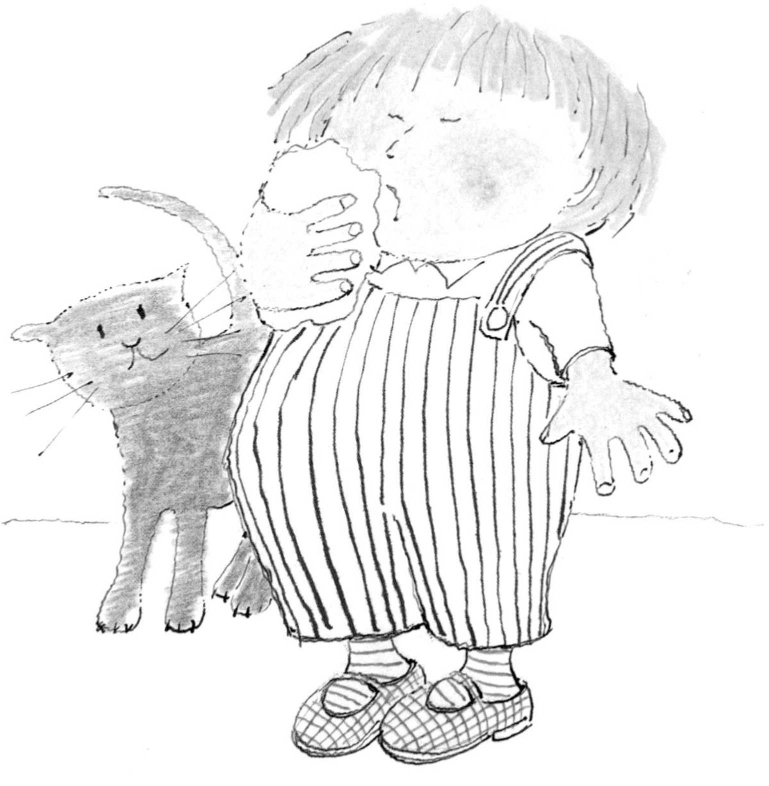

whisper

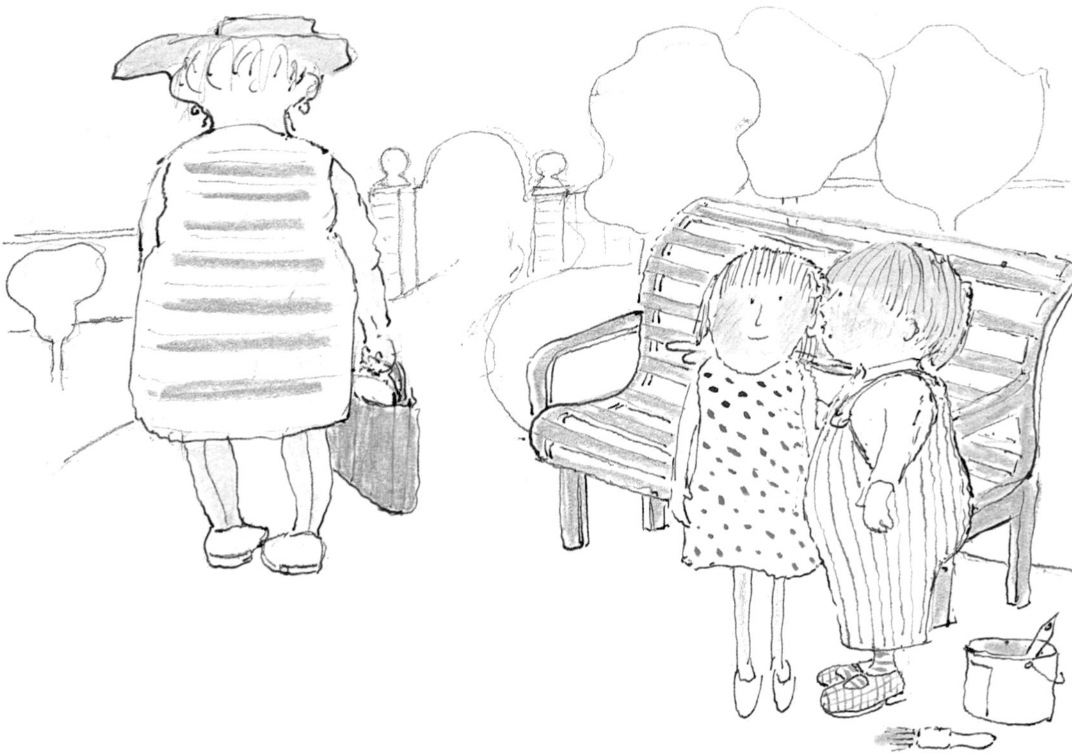

giggle

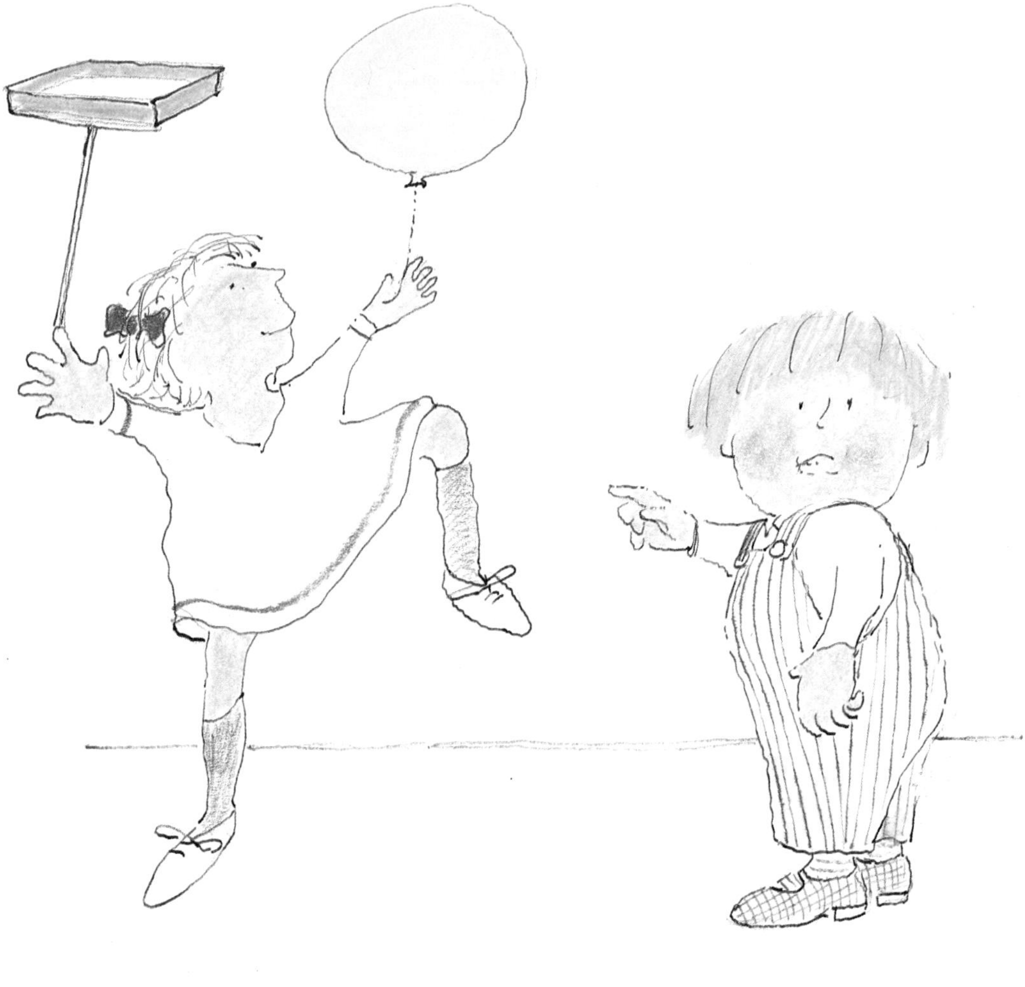

whistle

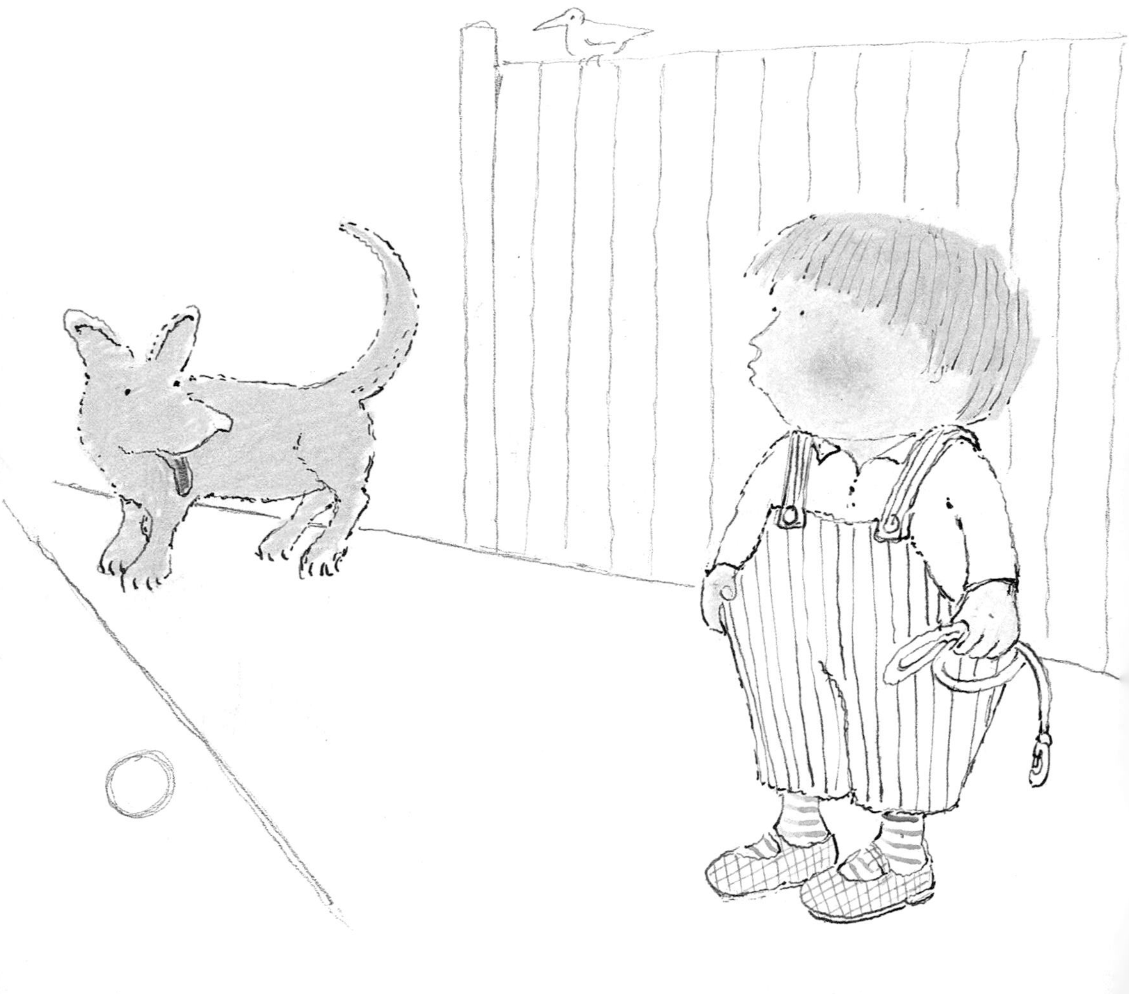

scratch

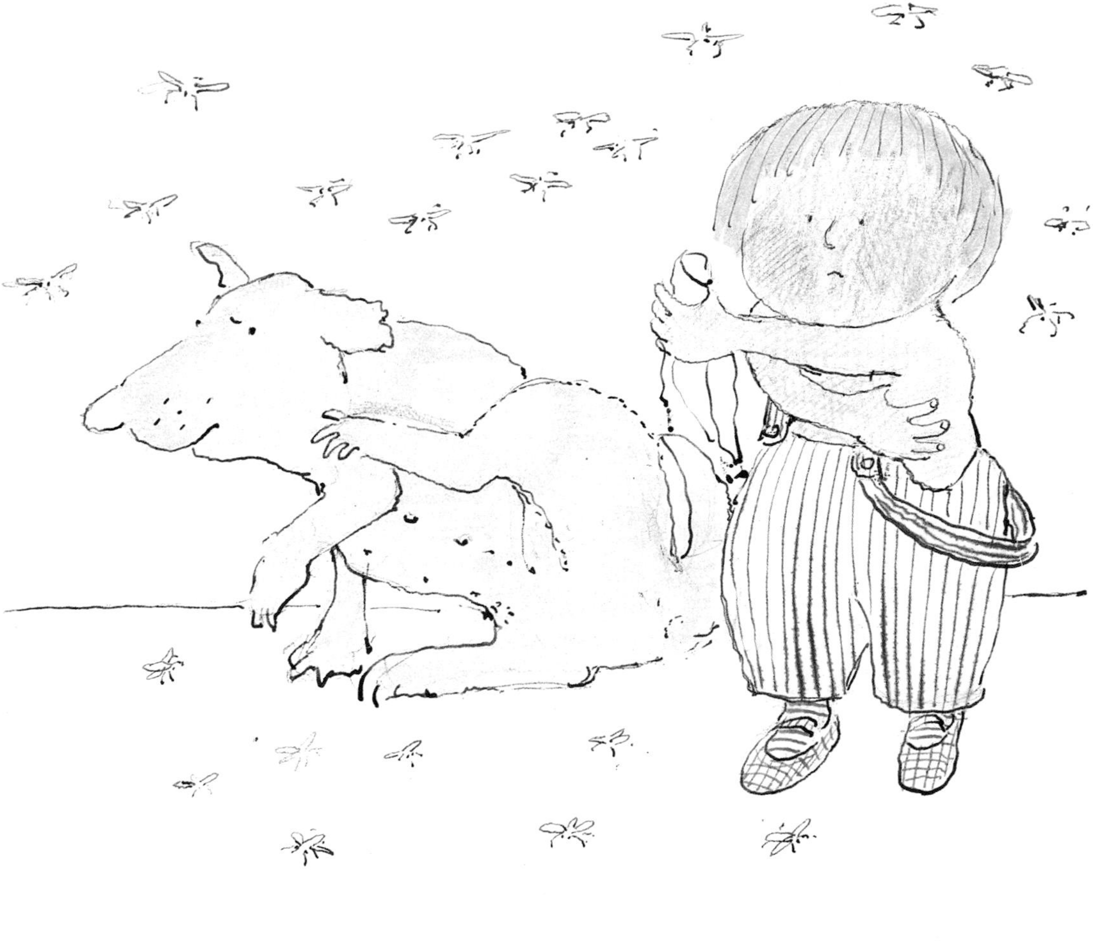

lick

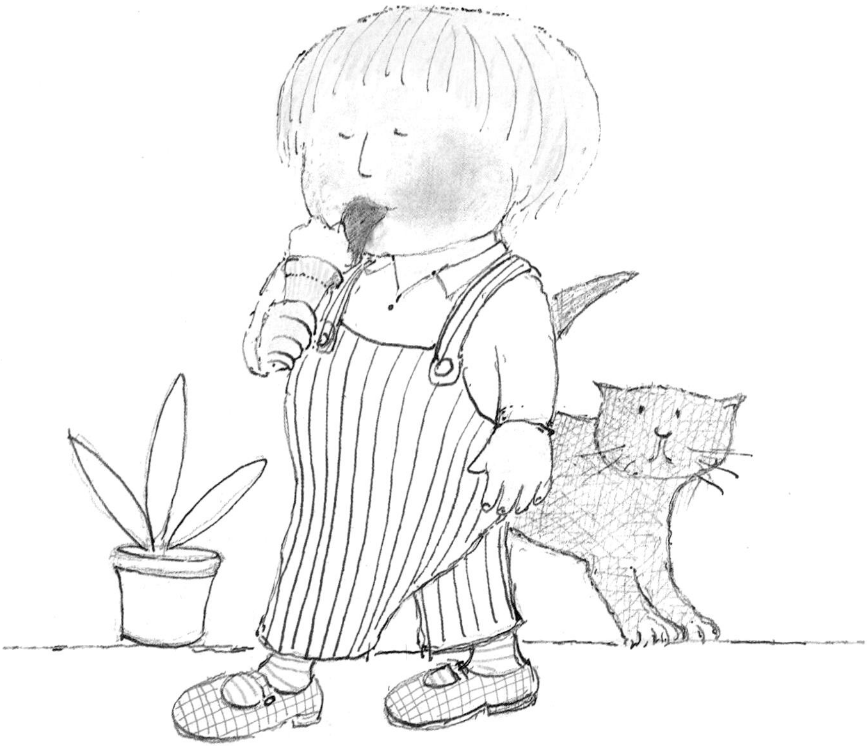

flap

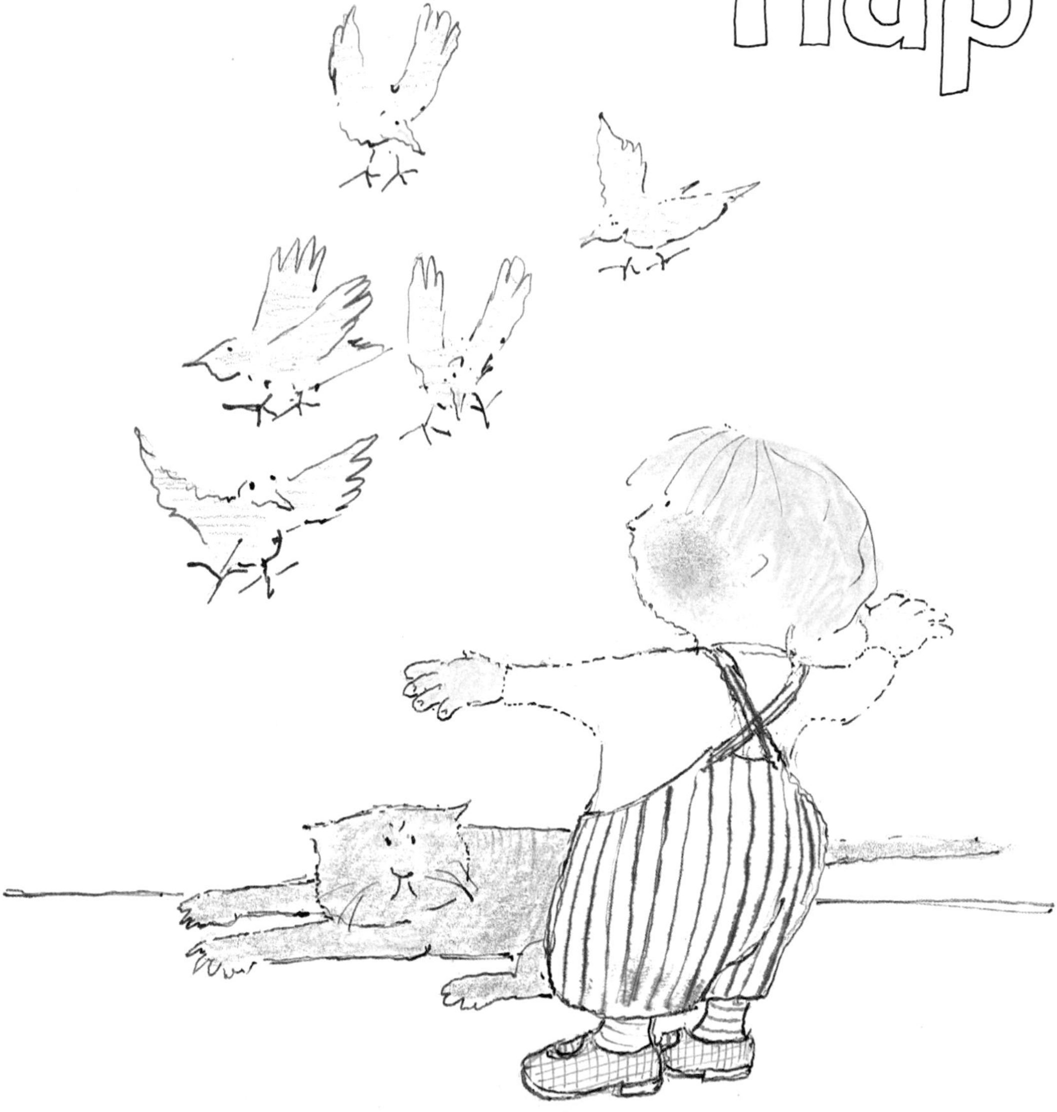

yawn

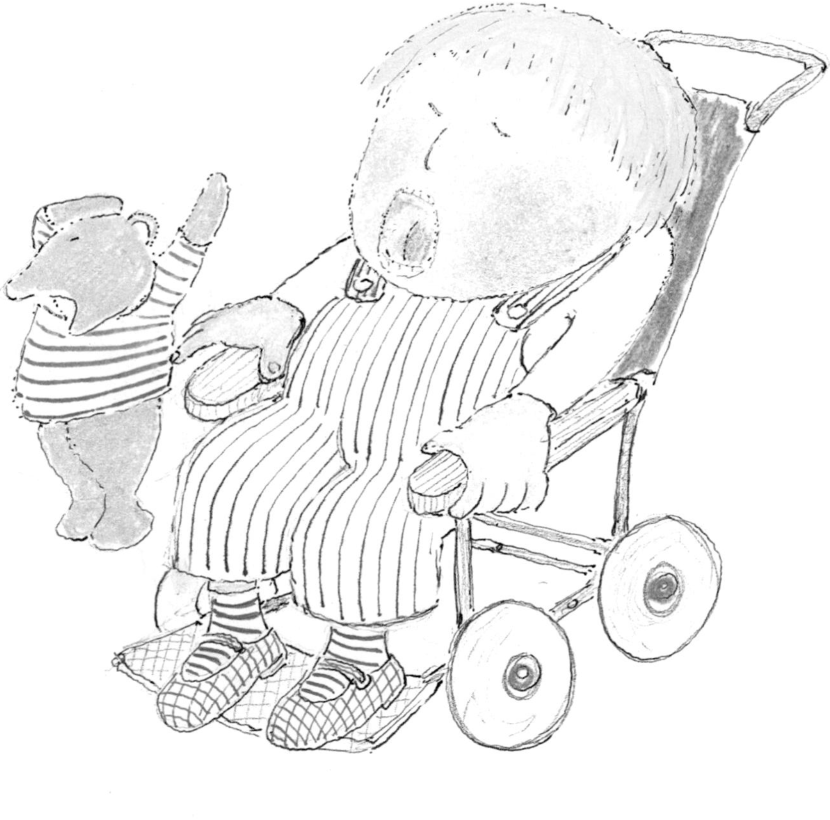

gargle

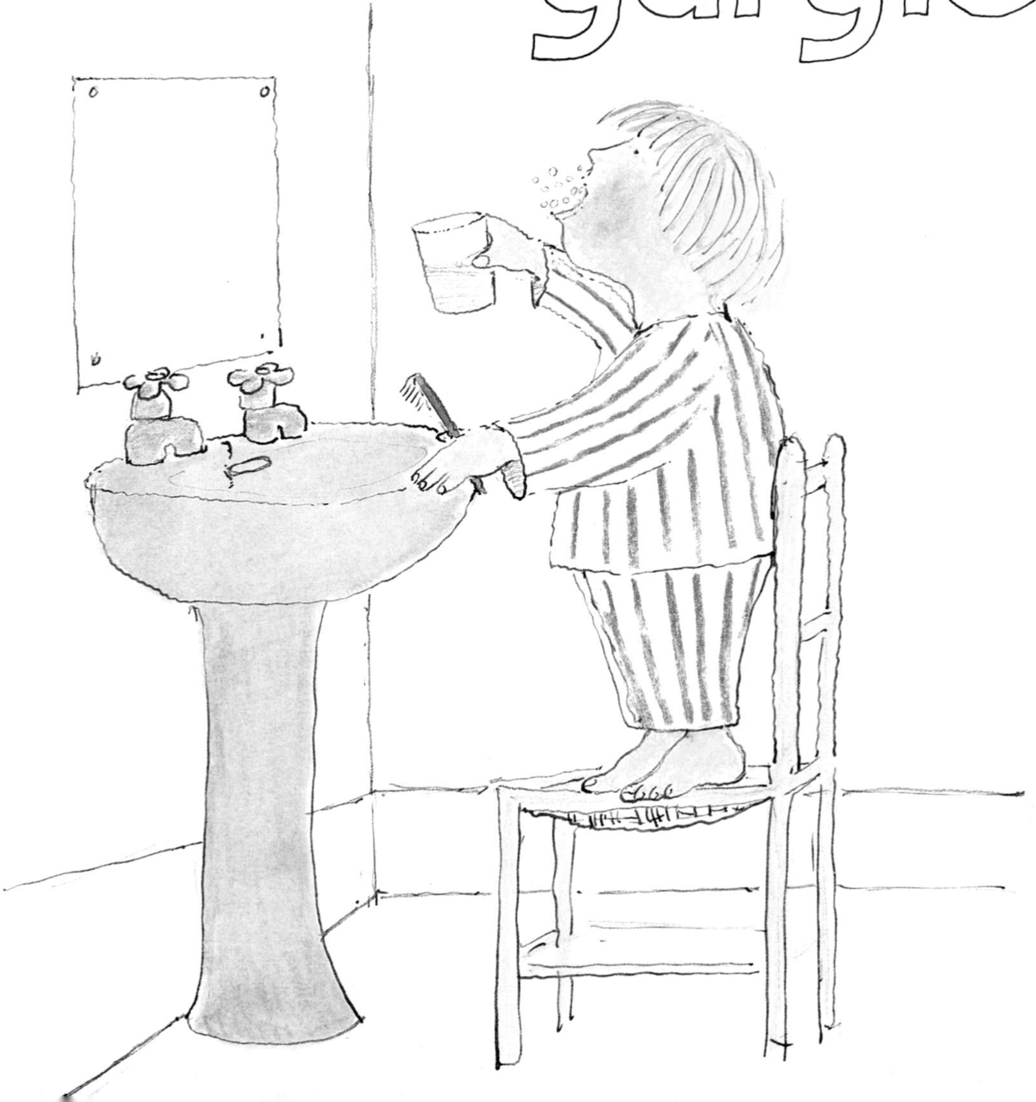

abcdefghijklmn